THIS BOOK IS DEDICATED TO MY THREE AMAZING CHILDREN FOR WHOM I WROTE IT AS A SONG FIFTEEN YEARS AGO.
KEEP PURSUING AND LIVING YOUR DREAMS MY LOVES, AND NEVER FORGET TO EMBRACE AND CHERISH YOUR JOURNEY

There once was a
dinosaur
Who didn't know how to roar
He tried and tried each day,
But no roar came his way

His friends would try to help
He'd start out with a yelp

And if the yelp grew loud,
His friends would all be
proud

But he would always
dream
To be just like his
team
Of Dinos playing
ball,
Roaring with
them all

His mom would say with zest,
Just do your very best
Your roar will come to be
Trust me,
you will see

Then he came upon
A teeny tiny dog
And all those in the
park
Were shocked by his
big bark

Inspired by what he saw,
He shook the doggie's
paw,
And tried and tried
again,
To roar across the land

He took a deep breath in
He knew it was in him

He roared from deep
inside
And shook the ground
with pride

Soon he was well known
From New York
through to Rome
The whole world's
greatest roar
Came from this dinosaur

He did his very best,
Forgot about the rest,
And his roar came to be
Try it
You will see
ROAR!!

JOYCE DAVIS